## PRAISE F

CW01645902

'From the backstreets

bakeries of Jette, Brussels, to cruising at thirty thousand feet – Du Bois takes you through the most tender, nostalgic, and sometimes grief-stricken moments of her life in an anthology of impeccably recounted flavour souvenirs. Where her familial tongues of Hokkien or French or Afrikaans have not sufficed, food is the language that fills her mouth. A deliciously fluent stroll – 'makan angin', eating air – with the characters and conversations that shape the poet's food memories.'

JENNY LAU

'*Eating Air* is a short but beautifully sweet (and savoury) evocation of food – its travels, connections and intimacies across time and space. Formally inventive, these poems are also both richly sensuous and wonderfully concrete in their explorations of eating, family and love.'

HANNAH LOWE

'In *Eating Air,* food becomes an archive, carrying whole geographies of longing. Tender, sensuous, and quietly devastating, these poems trace how taste can preserve what is fleeting, and how memory nourishes the body.'

ROMALYN ANTE

'Bittersweet, burning, intricate – these poems slip through languages and timezones to hold the weight of our hunger. Each poem like a fruit with textured skin, Suyin Du Bois writes with a sharpness that peels back layers of memory to reveal heat and longing at the core.'

NINA MINGYA POWLES

'Precise and fulsome in its appetites and attentions – in this beautiful book, food becomes a prism for every kind of relationship.'

WILL HARRIS

'This pamphlet is a beautiful exploration of identity, where food gets to be a way into complicated and complex storytelling that is generous and tender. Suyin Du Bois' writing tangles and untangles identity in a delicious way, that allows the reader to feel transported, whilst also seeing an inner story of self.'

ANNA SULAN MASING

# Eating Air

*Poems by Suyin Du Bois*

OTHER BOOKS FROM THE EMMA PRESS

POETRY PAMPHLETS

*Milk & Moon-water*, by Milena Williamson

*Noon*, by Zain Rishi

*Masters*, by Mark Ward

POETRY COLLECTIONS

*The Way the Water Held Me*, by Catherine Redford

*Daughter of the Sun*, by Rachel Spence

*Europe, Love Me Back*, by Rakhshan Rizwan

NOVELS

*The Waiter*, by Kwan Ann Tan

*Wild Boar*, by Hannah Lutz, trans. from Swedish by Andy Turner

ESSAY COLLECTIONS

*Bound: A Memoir of Making and Remaking*, by Maddie Ballard

*How Kyoto Breaks Your Heart*, by Florentyna Leow

*Tiny Moons: A Year of Eating in Shanghai*, by Nina Mingya Powles

SHORT STORY COLLECTIONS

*About Us*, by Reda Gaudiamo, translated from Indonesian by Ikhda Ayuning Maharsi Degoul and Philippa Barker

*Parables, Fables, Nightmares*, by Malachi McIntosh

POETRY AND ART SQUARES

*The Strange Egg*, by Kirstie Millar, illus. by Hannah Mumby

*The Fox's Wedding*, by Rebecca Hurst, illus. by Reena Makwana

BOOKS FOR CHILDREN

*Aardvark Day*, by Victoria Gatehouse, illus. by Kate Lucy Foster

*Poems from a Witch's Pocket*, by Laura Theis, illus. by Kate Lucy Foster

*Please Don't Read the Footnotes Please*, by Rob Walton, illustrated by Reena Makwana

# Eating Air

Poems by

Suyin Du Bois

Suyin x

THE EMMA PRESS

*For everyone who loves to go chiak hong or makan angin, gossips between mouthfuls about past and future meals, or longs to share food with people who are far away.*

THE EMMA PRESS

First published in the UK in 2026 by The Emma Press Ltd.
Poems © Suyin Du Bois 2026.

All rights reserved.

The right of Suyin Du Bois to be identified as the author of this work has been asserted in accordance with the Copyright, Designs and Patents Act 1988.
ISBN 978-1-915628-53-4

A CIP catalogue record of this book is available from the British Library.

Cover design by Reena Makwana.
Edited by James Trevelyan.
Typeset by Emma Dai'an Wright.

Printed and bound by CMP Digital Print Solutions, Poole.

The Emma Press
theemmapress.com
hello@theemmapress.com
Birmingham, UK

EU GPSR Authorised Representative
Logos Europe, 9 rue Nicolas Poussin,
17000, La Rochelle, France
E-mail: contact@logoseurope.eu

# CONTENTS

# PREFACE

Unusually for someone writing about food, I don't consider myself a keen cook. I probably can't tell you what spices are hiding in a spoonful of sauce I've just tasted. I love food more simply: for everything it makes me feel, everyone it connects me to, and of course, for the pure pleasure of eating. Given my Chinese-Malaysian and Belgian heritage, perhaps this isn't too surprising. They do say that Belgian cuisine achieves French quality in German portion sizes, and it is quite ordinary to be food-obsessed in Malaysia. *Chiak pah ah boey? Have you eaten yet?* Our typical greeting in Penang Hokkien positions wellbeing in the stomach, while *chiak hong* in Hokkien and *makan angin* in Malay – idioms for going on holiday or relaxing – translate literally to *eating air*. Visits back to both homes have always had a food checklist: moules-frites at Chez Léon, assam laksa opposite the Chinese Girls' School, peeling a caramelised Vigaufra from its paper whilst strolling the Rue Neuve, tambun biscuits and kaya to bring back to the UK. There is always something I'm longing for, no matter where in the world I am or have been.

When this longing became heightened during lockdown, my thoughts focused not only on the foods themselves, but also on the people, places and sensations I so vividly associated with them. It became clear that food is often at the core of what makes me feel I'm home, both physically and emotionally. Yet sometimes the very meal I've been craving to achieve that feeling becomes an othering experience. Based on my face, a hawker stall helper might bring me a fork for my noodles, or more distant aunties might be shocked that I can eat local ingredients with a more acquired taste like bitter gourd or petai, also known as stinky bean. As a result, I can often find myself in positions where I feel my identity is challenged through or around food, and I have a choice to assert it or not. *Chopsticks are fine* (I've been using them all my life). *I love these dishes* (I grew up eating them). Even in midlife, I am still learning how to navigate these moments.

As I recognised these complexities, each different meal felt like a new way into relationships or into myself, and the page felt like the perfect place to explore this. I was delighted every time I came across other food poems, saving away favourites like 'Ode to a Pot Noodle' by Romalyn Ante, 'Sausages' by Hannah Lowe, 'Refrigerator, 1957' by Thomas Lux, 'Persimmon abecedarian' by Cynthia Miller, and 'July' by Cristin O'Keefe Aptowicz, amongst others. Reading and writing about food began to feel as delicious as sitting down to eat. I found that certain combinations of words can have just the right mouthfeel, like the silky stickiness of Greek yoghurt and honey. Reading a poem out loud can bring me into my body, the way that sitting down to a meal can. I have to remind myself to slow down, pay attention, chew each mouthful twenty times – a trick I play to get myself out of my head, where I spend so much of my time. I learned that through condensing a moment into thirtyish lines of its most central flavours, it solidifies somewhere inside me as it does on the page. Would you believe that the nasi lemak Malaysia Airlines serves for breakfast two hours before touchdown tastes more like coming home to me now that I've written a poem about it?

In this way, the poems in these pages form a part of my ongoing endeavour to answer the question of my belonging, journeying back and forth across the world, pausing to chiak hong in all the places I call home.

# *Ode to Kaya*

*Egg jam* first on my young tongue: palm sugar
sweet, coconut milk rich. Thick layers on charred
toast, salted butter cubes between, melting in Penang
sweat. My Goh Ee Poh stood for hours stirring you
in that double-boiled heat. Exports to be swaddled,
twisted into pink and green plastic bags, nestled
amongst swimming costumes and sundresses – rituals
to ward off mid-air leaks in the 14 hours from one home
to the other. Back in England your layers thinned,
our knives more sparing after each spread.
After Goh Ee Poh grew too frail, aunties and uncles
gifted us store-bought surrogates. You were labelled *Kaya.*
Our cupboards filled with your empties, aides-mémoire
of indulgence repurposed to house fragrant rice, Chinese
mushrooms, our longing for Nyonya flavours.

By the time pandan leaves arrive in Chinatown, I am grown
up, have my own kitchen where I can stand for hours.
Goh Ee Poh has long since condensed
into photographs, so I sweeten my never-asked
regret, trace down someone else's heirloom recipe.
You are needy, threaten lumps, failure, but I stir and stir
like her until my spoon draws the right depths of lineage.
I lift a heap of you into my mouth, tongue
your clotted grainy sweetness.

# *Omelette or Nasi Lemak?*

Cabin lights flick on, shades slide up
to the Bay of Bengal's dusky orange glow.
I blink awake, groggy and fur-toothed,
orient myself by the rattle of the trolley cart.
Lifting the fruit tray first, I welcome the familiar
chill sting of melon cubes on my front teeth.
Next the yoghurt pot that spurts no matter
how I whisper the foil back. *Tuan-tuan dan puan-puan*
over the tannoy speeds me home. I spoon sambal,
scatter peanuts, ikan bilis over the egg poised
on my rice, assemble each mouthful just so
and, like that, it's no longer plane food.
It's the Sri Weld sambal my cousin Nicky jokes
is extra spicy whenever the hawker has a scowl on.
It's pyramids from Auntie Lin we carry to the beach,
swinging plastic bags tight around our fingers
so we can scoop sheeny red-stained rice
with our backs resting on boulders – so lemak.
It's breakfast with Joël at Ah Wang where stray cats
watch us for crumbs or kindness, and we unfold
banana leaves beside half-boiled eggs and kaya toast –
an indulgence my brother agrees is worth the detour.

I fold my napkin into my meal tray.
What a substantial appetiser. How well
the cabin crew has prepared me for landing.
When Joël asks at Arrivals, *Are you hungry?*
My answer will still be *Yes*.

## *The First Mouthful*

In the back corner of Pulau Tikus market, tucked in
behind uncles pressing fresh santan, trays of kueh
steamed overnight, gutted fish, beside batik dresses
and the energetic ladling of hawker sellers, I sit still –
watch tiny bubbles on the surface of my koay teow th'ng.

I'm not sure what's woken me so early: jet lag
or my stomach aching for hot soup in the heat, for kopi
strong and Carnation-swirled, for the kinship of their steam.

I pull fine white noodles from the broth's well-oiled clarity,
wind them into the flat base of my spoon, chopstick up:
a slither of duck, crunchy pork lard, one wide-blinked
iris of chilli padi to top the pile. Nudging the spoon back
into the liquid so it wells up around this first mouthful,
I catch the curious eye of the uncle at the next table.

*Where are you from?*
                                        *Wah eh mama si Penang lang.*
The words mis-intoned, or too unexpected
from this face, he frowns.

The rooster on the side of my bowl hasn't yet crowed me
fully awake, so I say *London* and we both smile. I turn back,
slurp my spoonful down – feel the quick slip of the koay teow,
the stock radiating through me, the chilli biting at my throat.

# *Cut Scenes*

Dad fusses with his leather school bag / before sitting down to breakfast / by the coal-fired stove / in a 1920s maison de ville I've visited from the pavement / my grand-père / who I know from Agfa Billy snaps of walking holidays in the Ardennes / Sunday best studio portraits / has sizzled him a small steak / in a lump of butter / crisped at the edges / deep juicy red in the centre / fried bread on the side / the best way he knows / to sustain his son / on the bundled walk across the tram tracks to school / to protect him / against its respected priests / the wooden blackboard erasers they aim at boys' heads

Dad orders steak in a restaurant / *blue* / *walking to the table* / *by the excuse-me method of cooking* / one part joke / three parts recipe / waiters don't always get it / my held breath / a kind of grace / I watch for his knife to deliver / deep juicy red / not pink / worse grey / how else / can he see his father again / only when I know / it won't be sent back / I slice my own / reveal / the fibres that make us

# *Brussels on the Eve of Lockdown*

We'd bring it even if it weren't her birthday:
duty-free Moët for Jeanne's 95th. Clink together
her champagne coupes with a *tchin tchin!* Make an occasion
of any afternoon. There are so few pleasures
for the housebound. Leaning in around her
low marble table, we float the glasses down, mindful
of their fine rims' survival through a century or more
of family toasts. All around us are photographs of ourselves:
babies then toddlers on her lap in the same chair she sits in
today, embraced by huge scroll armrests that outsized us then,
now her. She's not with us at our graduations or weddings,
but the photographs jostle for room across every surface.
In the hand of an elegant antique figure, she keeps
an ugly plastic and paper flower I made for her
as a child. My brother speaks fluently
for us both. My tongue trips over French words
I believe I know. I want so much to answer
better, ask more. Why does she always say
*tchin tchin*, never *santé*? How long
have these glasses been in our family? Did she ever
want children of her own? The alcohol doesn't untwist
my tongue. She never stops trying
to speak to me, her eyebrows raised, eyes expectant
through my fumbled replies. *Je suis désolée*. We stay long
after the sun stops catching the purple relief
of the Val Saint Lambert vase on the sill, delaying the moment

we'll kiss her goodbye, feel the fine skin of her cheek shift
softly against ours three times. The apartment gets dark.
I cradle my coupe in my palm, trace
the etched loops encircling its widest point.

# *Beginner Hokkien, but Fluent in Kueh*

Before speaking, this nose introduces me
to the party as European, not Penang lang.
Yet this feast of kueh allows me a way in.
Pandan leaf, butterfly pea flower, dark beet,
coconut flesh mingle on the Lazy Susan swirled
between guests. We sate silence with stories
of firm favourites and elusive treats we long for,
whose sweetness still coats our cheeks.

> A handful of sellers at Pulau Tikus:
> onde onde from the elderly uncle by night,
> ang koo kueh from the early morning stalls.
> The Seremban auntie who sells her pulut inti
> on Saturdays at the Putney Thameside charms
> a queue of kaki lang seeking that warm balm
> you lick off banana leaf ridges.

No one realises I have memorised these Nyonya
names, that each time I return I find them hanging
glutinous, caramelised, ready to celup
my half ang moh mouth.
Not *the green and white layer one,*
not *the burnt tapioca one,*
not *the kaya one.*
Kueh talam, kueh beng kah, pulut tai tai.

# *Craving Eng Chai, I Detour to Chinatown*

In the fluorescent stage light of a Gerrard Street grocery
a pile of slender leaves serenades me with its many names:
eng chai, ong choy, kangkong, water spinach, morning glory.
I can already taste it – earthy, baritone under sambal belacan,
fermented tofu, garlic and oyster sauce. Despite the price tag
of its emigration, I take a bundle home, rinse small palmfuls
under a running tap. Scorpions hid in the hollow stems of Mum's
old sinkside warning: a Sungai Petani rural legend losing its sting
as it's passed from a near-forgotten auntie to Ah Mah to Mum
to me. What should make me want to drown those leaves
brings me closer to the mud of the harvest, to hands
bold like mine. In the right conditions, a simple cutting
could flourish. I feel for a node, proof of roots, fantasise
four metres of stalks stretching across my patch
of London clay from camellia to wisteria, thriving
in puddles, singing themselves to the sun
between overcast days.

# *Auntie Pixi's Aga Agak*

Your precise handwriting, every time I open my fridge:
*RHUBARB & MANGO May 2018*. Behind this label
remnants of old ones peek out. We're so particular

in this family. I don't know your criteria
for jam jars, but I know not to give you any new ones;
join the tide of handing back empty, receiving full.

*SARA* is scored into the metal lid of this one, a vestige
of your daughter's boarding school tuck that dates it
back to leg warmers and Wham!

Who else has strained to pop it open?
How long after you arrived here
did you find your first gelling point?

Between acting jobs as immigrant nurses,
a student waving Mao's Little Red Book, an elderly
assassin so small and deadly, you've worked 35-hour weeks

in your English country garden – riding your lawnmower,
weed-pulling with such vigour you snap tendons in your hand.
When your rhubarb is at its best in May or June,

you get the pans boiling on your Aga, simmer
until these temperate and tropical fibres fuse.
Like you, I reuse carrier bags and revel

in unfranked stamps, so I make every jar you give me last.
When Sara calls with the news that will make this jar
  the last,
it becomes too precious to dip into. We drink tea

under the care home's wisteria as you guesstimate
the hours of pruning in their beds and pergolas, the rhubarb
going unpicked in your own. You reach for the sweetener

tucked in your fleece pocket and I half expect you
to pull out a pair of secateurs. I struggle
to believe you've only weeks left. To pre-empt

my regret, I fit in as many questions as I can.
When I ask for the recipe you say *It's just fruit and jam sugar,*
no measurements or method. You trust I can figure it out.

# *On the First Cold Day of Winter, You Ask for Rusks*

Tannie Noeline's recipe calls for true
boeremeisie quantities, so I adapt

each measure by awkward fractions –
still the batter laps the lip of my bowl

as I wed flour to crushed bran to buttermilk.
The last step says *Dry*. I had to google it

the first time and, even on the thirteenth,
I worry when to take them out of the oven,

leave them in overnight. In the morning,
our house smells of a hunger that's spread

wide since our last trip back to your childhood home,
my windfall one. We don't wait. We dunk

rough chopped rusks into our coffee and you tell me
once more about your ouma's aniseed beskuit,

so tall and arid they'd absorb half a mug
in one dip, hang sodden only long enough for your mouth

to get under their fall. We reminisce about road trips
between Hermanus and Bothaville, how I make us pause

at every padstal, seek out the most tempting treats
– banana and bran, pumpkin seed and apricot –

how every homemade rusk tempts us. You remind me
that mine are your favourite, and I reply *Jy is my gunsteling*.

And we keep going until the bottom of our mugs is a beach
of sunflower seeds and crumbs with the tide sucked out.

# *WhatsApps with Mum*

Look
at this hopefully delicious
custard apple from Taiwan.

Look
at this humongous fig
I found in Rome, from Puglia.
Dessert spoon for scale!

It's buah chiku. We had a huge tree
at Number 25, but the fruits
were smaller and browner.

Tried fresh cacao fruit at a plantation today.
Barely any flesh around the seed,
tastes a little like lychee.

Bought a kilo of duku at a rest stop.
They gave me a fruit called rambai to try.
Interesting, similar to duku,
but has a more sour note.
Good for us, says The Internet.

Bought a sweaty bag of boiled
pejibayes in Quepos. Locals eat it with
mayo and strong coffee for breakfast.
Lots of peeling.
Substantial, fibrous, and savoury.

Guess what this is?!

Do you know this very ugly fruit? It's called noni.
Very good for you in a smoothie I'm told,
but you must mix it with something else. Ominous.
Google says its other name is vomit fruit…

Having durian for dinner –
started with Red Prawn,
following up with Butter King.

Lijynn got me miracle fruit
from Balik Pulau. The miracle is
it blocks your sour tastebuds.
Tested it with some Greek yoghurt.
It works!

Don't you think this looks like snake skin?
It's called buah salak or snake skin fruit.
Not too sweet. Flesh firm and crunchy.

Custard apples at Borough for £4.80, uggh!!

Coming to drop off strawberries
from Ying's allotment around 3:30.

A mulberry tree in Calvinia,
fruit too high sadly. Made me think
of the dried ones you love
from that Persian shop in Peckham.

Got this custard apple to share with you.
It wasn't ripe enough and now it's too ripe.

Do you know milk fruit or abiu?
Refreshing and sweet,
faint taste of persimmon.
I'll get one for us to share.

# *Super Nutty Wholefood*

Mum and I crunch precise slices
of green bean. We ruminate
broccoli florets between our teeth. Quinoa,
pistachio, almond. The plastic container
promises *I am good for you.*
Nurses talk of CABG and I see
surgeons coring the withered
segments of Dad's heart. They transplant
raw brassica leaves snapped fresh
off the stem – their bright, pulsing
veins arch out, oxygenate
his crinkled edges. Chocolate digestives
next to the kettle, shortcrust quiches
Nazia bakes as comfort –
I scorn them all. André eats my share
and I prickle, *You really having that?*
I should say I mean to grow old
together, don't ever want any one of us
back here: intubated or hanging on
for news under these cold tube lights.
I insist we oil our bloodlines
mackerel slick, enough omega-3 to counter
the hospital's menu: stacked trolleys
of Full English bacon and sausages
glue as they cool, loaded mac & cheese
congeals, custard on sticky toffee pudding
films over. I remind everyone how fat hardens
around the heart.

# *Don't Like to Get My Hands Dirty*

Serve me chicken wings, I'll choose a knife and fork
every time. Can't stand sauce on handles, a cloud
of sticky prints on glass. Where the dirt might end up
later. What it might contaminate.
Don't worry. The bones I leave behind sucked smooth,
cartilage crunched off. Constraints make me
a problem-solver. If we're sharing king prawns, I'll dig
my thumbnail under their carapaces, pull off heads,
ease delicate fins of flesh from the thinnest ends
of their tails. Challenge myself to do it
without breaking. The impulse to smooth
a rogue hair from my forehead grows
unbearable, but I won't touch my face with these hands.
Can't wait to soap off the gunk. I monitor
my friends' fingers, watch for tiny flecks flung
in my direction as they talk and laugh and peel.
Not everyone cordons off their world by degrees
of cleanliness.
                                        But bring me to George Town. Settle me
at a marble table, cool and clean against my forearms.
Seat me at a stool low enough for my feet to rest,
where I tuck one ankle under the other thigh like Mum
says Ah Mah did beneath her sarong kebaya.
Let me serve my cousin Nicky spoonfuls of sambal petai
as she dishes me jiu hu char – its fine shredded
cuttlefish, jicama, mushroom, pork belly, sweated down
to luscious mess. I will be the first to pick a crisp cup

of lettuce, still wet from washing, fill it, dab on sambal,
parcel up the leaf, its whitest parts snapping, sweet juice
running down my fingers past the web of my hand.
I will lick it off the base of my palm and reach for another.

# *After Six Weeks of Counting Macros*

I spread my holiday butter thicker,
mirror my in-laws' melting smears
on a fourth slice of ouma brood. We collude
on calories, agree our morning walk
through Balkfontein's dusted streets
means we need the energy. I split
with Tannie the avocado *the boys* don't like,
emphasise the long *aai* of my *baie lekker*,
fill my convivial mouth with another bite
of fig and pecan mascarpone they recall
I loved so much last time. Abundant
creamed crunch of those sweet seeds. I divvy
the marrowbones with Pa, balance
their rich core on the precarious tilt
of my knife. Stuffed, I finally refuse
another bite, press my lips together and listen
eyes-closed to the off-key mumbles of my gut
and my heart. Why do I accept
every delicacy offered, when I must
tame my cholesterol, when I want
to share morning walks with family
through all my years? I keep cool
under the stoep's tin roof, sun slanting
at my ankles, and join the chorus
of satisfied *mmms* around the table. I can forgive
this well-mannered grease bonding
in my veins. I can thumb the belt loops free
from my belly.

# *Mum Peels and Pops a Sand-Roasted Chestnut Into My Mouth,*

still warm and creamy from the roadside stall
beside Chowrasta that we treat
like a drive-through: wind down our window
to let the aircon blend with the charred aroma
clinging to the humid street air, call out
to the uncle for a 10-ringgit scoop.

Another mum strolling towards us
with two teenage girls, spots
the paper bag, Mum's fingertips
blackened oily from peeling,
the glossy kernel disappearing
into my mouth.

*Ooooh… jealous!* she teases.

I turn towards joy, do a little food jiggle,
and Mum, not missing the wink
of opportunity, peels and pops one
into this other mum's mouth.

If those girls roll their eyes as I would've
once – so embarrassed by Mum
stopping a stranger to compliment
their handbag or ask unnecessary
directions to practise her Spanish –
then I don't see it. I'm already past them,
with Mum in full view and filled
with the giddy combination of our laughter,
the gentlest brown sugar high.

# *Three Anak Campur Meet at George Town Lit Fest*

and seek out a bar hidden behind shophouse shutters
we shimmy open. *Good Friends Never Bojio.*
We spent the afternoon workshopping our writing:

memories of after-school shopping trips
through towering grocery store aisles with a beloved
late uncle, musings on moments that stretch out

awkward between new acquaintances waiting
for food to arrive. The three of us filled silences
full before hawkers could find us with brimming bowls

of laksa and bak kut teh. So many shared frustrations
over Grab drivers who ask why I have a Chinese name,
where in the Middle East Haneen is from, question

why her Malay is so good, dig to uncover
Andrew's British-Thai grandmother. How easily we belong
to each other – like the cucumber and pineapple gin

in Haneen's spicy negroni, Andrew's jujube-infused Campari,
my Milo-less Milo cocktail of cacao whisky, Guinness
and parmesan. Everything is campur-campur, and so sedap.

# *Dinner and a Movie*

Into our lazy Nissin noodle dinner
we drop dumplings straight from the freezer,

submerge tender pak choi leaves and stems.
Childhood food for me. You name it *future food* –

turn us into Aunt Beru and Uncle Owen
in our whitewash Tatooine kitchen,

worrying about Luke and those new droids
while something beeps and bubbles around us.

Bowls steaming into our faces, we dive in
with chopsticks, pull on as many strands

as we can. We don't discuss our leaky roof,
the colleague who's winding you up, instead perch

beside Deckard in downtown LA, shelter
from rain in all that Vaporwave. You suggest

new lives in off-world colonies,
slip adventure into my weeknights.

# *Every Trip to Brussels Must Include a Sunday*

For the marché de Jette / For queuing at Sirre with the high-stakes decision / couque au beurre or pain au chocolat / For *both* being an acceptable decision / For sitting in the sun avec un petit café with its reliable speculoos / For peering into the old Bossuyt bakery / wondering how much / of the cabinetry is the original crafted by my arrière-grand-père / For Mum / taking us into Neuhaus en famille to treat us to her favourite / Irrésistibles / bending over the glass counter / dithering over dark / milk / nuts / fresh raspberry cream / For the patient shop assistant who hands us each an extra piece on the house / For the market trader I must track down / who sells just one kind of pastry / the name of which I can never remember / For Dad reminding me / every time / For walking past where La Carretta was / reminiscing how we spent New Year's Eves there / mid-conga line / with paper hats and streamers and perms and tulle party dresses / their ruffled mesh grazing my outstretched palms as I twirl / For américain préparé and salade de céleri-rave / For remembering / the shopkeeper at the old traiteur l'Ardennais with the beautiful bass voice singing out *Bonjour Mesdames* / as Mum and I return / *Bonjour Monsieur!* / For Dad lamenting *The market has gotten smaller / it used to spread much further down these roads from the Miroir* / For the market being the same size for as long as I can remember / For telling / strangers / *Je dois pratiquer mon français* / For asking again / which kind of maatjes was Jeanne's favourite / For plums / clementines / strawberries / whatever is in season and plentiful / For debating with Mum / *Are we buying too much* / For agreeing we can manage it / between us / For Joël hanging back to perfectly line up photos of Trappist cheese wedges or glossy éclairs / For the towering rotisserie lorry and its wall of charring chicken / For Dad to check out the latest bandes dessinées / For noticing more stalls with baklava / olives / baba ganoush / For the new Thai food truck / For spotting custard apples for the first time / For pomegranates / persimmons and figs / pared open for you to taste / For Mum always tasting / For André choosing too many sauces for his cone at the fritkot / For ballotins at Leonidas / one for while we're here / a few to carry back as gifts / one or two more for ourselves / For layers / of fresh cream manons for Dad / For succumbing / For resisting / as we inhale rich griddled butter from galettes pressed crisp in the iron / For returning the vidange that Mum and Dad stored all year in the understairs cupboard and rattled over in the boot of the car / For realising / the stalls are wrapping up / For dividing / conquering / For meeting again in front of Sirre / For the clothes and homewares we never buy / remind me of pasar malam / earmarking every Tuesday night for nasi ulam at Tanjung Bungah / before I leave again / For pink nose tips from browsing too long in the cold / For crowding around tall tables at the edge of the Place du Miroir so we can warm up with a late-morning tipple and caricoles in peppery broth / For feeling overindulged and like it's never enough

# *Market Day in Monte San Savino*

In have-a-go Italian, we learn
these first-harvest apricots
*sono cari ma i più dolci.*
To prove it, the trader splits one
with just her fingers, bears perfect
even halves. Flesh so tender
the stone falls free, hangs
by a single fibre. What is this sorcery?
She hands them over, and she is right.
No hint of an astringent edge. Its juice
floods my mouth, so floral and fragrant
I confuse it for a tiny peach.

Back at the agriturismo, I listen
to that soft voice that offers *Why not?*
The one I wish would let me
emigrate anyplace warmer,
where I can buy from growers'
hands and fruits have time
to ripen on the branch. I try my luck
at the trader's trick, line up my thumbs
either side of the fruit's soft furrow,
pull gently, and discover
it gives to me too.

# *Chinese New Year at Sara's*

I bring tau eu bak, Mum's recipe, simmered
for hours, pork belly part-melted to sauce,
dried mushrooms grown fat on soy.
*Cuz, you can really cook!* you hype me
with a squeeze to my forearm. You've made
a special trip to the Korean supermarket,
bought too much frozen dim sum again.
We pool our bamboo steamers, stack them
tall in your Hammersmith kitchen. Out steams
my favourite, har gau, your favourite, siu mai.
Mum and Dad are in KL this time of year
sending videos of 16 nights of fireworks,
up-high selfies trying to fit in all the family
at the banqueting table. Your mum's in Shropshire.
So all my adult life reunion dinner has been
with Big Cuz Sara, our husbands, your daughter.
Our *Chinese New Year* group chat pings year-round.
Last spring I told an auntie about our tradition
and she scolded us for doing it wrong. We should
toss together a bright abundance of crunchy
symbolism in yee sang, serve a whole fish
head to tail, slurp longevity noodles without biting.
We try not to take it as proof we're not Chinese
enough, decide we make our own meaning.
May we be as well-fed as the pig we're eating!
May our luck tower high as our steamers!
We layer on red to maximise our chances:

our jumpers, the lacquered chopstick rests
I gave you for Christmas, napkins to match,
my ang pow for your daughter, our ang moh
husbands, our blended blood.

# ACKNOWLEDGEMENTS

Thank you to all the wonderful poets I've been fortunate enough to read, listen to, learn from and be in community with.

To André for your unending patience and support, not least as my first listener, and for naming the dreams coming true (a book for me, liner notes for you).

To Mum, Dad, Joël and all my family near and far. To Sophie, Adam, Alick, Beaney, Dan, Elaine, Marisa, Phil and all my friends who've bought anthologies and attended readings.

To Emma Dai'an Wright, James Trevelyan, Georgia Wall, and The Emma Press team, also to Reena Makwana.

To my poetry and writing friends in London and around the world for your encouragement and inspiration: Helen Bowell, Hetty Cliss, Barbara Cooke, Salma Daneshmand, Haneen Martin, Mycah Miller, Serge Neptune, Nina Mingya Powles, Pratyusha, Jennifer Wong, the Ponchettes, Bubble Tea Writers, the PTDS community, BESEA Poets, and especially Lexi Pelle for your close editing over the last four years. To Will Harris, Vanessa Kisuule, Sophie Ransby and my fellow Peekists.

To Judith Palmer at the Poetry Society, Sean Wai Keung at Red Bean Poetry, Eduard Burle and Melissa Sussens at the Red Wheelbarrow, and Eva Wong Nava and Lucy Tandon Copp at StoryFeast for inviting me to read and speak at your events.

To Mary Jean Chan for *Propel*, Mark Antony Owen at *iamb*, Ben Townley-Canning for *Bi+ Lines: An Anthology of Contemporary Bi+ Poets* (Fourteen Publishing), Cia Mangat at *zindabad zine*, and Hayley Frances for Verve Poetry POTM for first publishing earlier versions of some of these poems.

## ABOUT THE POET

Suyin Du Bois is a poet of mixed Chinese-Malaysian and Belgian heritage, living in London with her South African husband. Her poems have been published in *Propel*, *Iamb*, *Stanzas*, *Bi+ Lines: An Anthology of Contemporary Bi+ Poets* (Fourteen Publishing, 2023) and *Malaysian Places and Spaces* (Maya Press, 2024), amongst others. She is a member of the Southbank Centre's New Poets Collective 2024/25. When not obsessing over word choice, Suyin spends her time building a profit-with-purpose start-up that seeks to ensure 24/7 access to nutritious, affordable food for NHS hospital staff. *Eating Air* is her debut pamphlet.

## ABOUT THE EMMA PRESS

The Emma Press is an independent publishing house based in Birmingham. It was founded in 2012 by Emma Dai'an Wright and specialises in poetry, short fiction and children's books, with translations across all genres.

Recent publications have won the Edge Hill Debut Short Story Prize and been shortlisted for the CLiPPA and the Week Junior Book Awards.

theemmapress.com
@TheEmmaPress